"BRING THE CLASSICS TO LIFE"

THE INVISIBLE MAN

LEVEL 3

Series Designer
Philip J. Solimene

Editor
Laura Machynski

EDCON

Long Island, New York

Story Adaptor
Richard D. Ferrie

Author
H. G. Wells

About the Author

Herbert George Wells was born on September 21, 1866, in Kent, England. His father, Joseph, owned a china and glass shop. He was also a professional bowler and coach for the Kent County Cricket Club. Joseph had an accident in 1877 which ended his professional career. This accident caused financial hardship for the family, and it was this tragedy that helped the Wells' marriage to fail. These difficulties forced young Herbert to leave school and make his own way in the world. He held many apprenticeships, but he believed in self-education. In his spare time he studied physiography, physiology, chemistry, and mathematics. In 1884, Herbert successfully obtained a scholarship to the Normal School of Science where he trained as a science teacher. It was here that he became editor of the school's journal where his first serious attempts at writing were published. In 1895, Wells opted for a full-time writing career and his first important short stories were published. His next work, *THE TIME MACHINE* received 'rave' reviews and thereafter, his popularity grew as a writer of science fiction. Some of his other works include *THE ISLAND OF DR. MOREAU, WAR OF THE WORLDS,* and *THE FIRST MEN IN THE MOON*. H. G. Wells died in 1946. He left behind many works filled with wonder and fascination.

Copyright © 1992
A/V Concepts Corp.
Long Island, New York

This book may be reproduced for student/classroom use.
All other rights reserved.

Printed in U.S.A.
ISBN# 1-55576-063-5

CONTENTS

Words Used 4, 5

NO.	TITLE	SYNOPSIS	PAGE
31	**The Strange Man**	Mrs. Hall has a strange-looking new guest staying at her hotel. Everyone in town wonders who he is and where he comes from. One day, Mrs. Hall gets a chance to see how strange her new guest *really* is!	6
32	**Flying Furniture!**	Mrs. Hall wants to learn more about the stranger. Upstairs in his room, she does some snooping. What she finds, sends her running from the hotel.	12
33	**Invisible!**	The stranger reveals his secret to Mrs. Hall and the crowd that has gathered at the hotel. Everyone learns that catching the stranger will not be an easy task.	18
34	**The Unhappy Helper**	The invisible man knows that, to live in his condition, he will need the help of another person. He enlists the help of a friendly hobo by means of physical force.	24
35	**More Fear in a New Town**	The invisible man and the hobo walk to another town. In need of money, the invisible man decides to rob a tavern. When Mr. Marvel hears about the theft, he runs through the town to warn the people of the invisible man's arrival.	30
36	**Dr. Kemp's Visitor**	Mr. Marvel runs to a nearby tavern for help. The invisible man follows, and someone at the tavern shoots him. Hurt and bleeding, the invisible man enlists the help of a friendly doctor to help him stay alive.	36
37	**Friend or Enemy?**	The invisible man tells Dr. Kemp that they had been good friends many years before. He asks the doctor for his help, and the doctor agrees. But secretly, Dr. Kemp warns the police of the invisible man's whereabouts.	42
38	**The Invisible Man's Story**	The invisible man tells Dr. Kemp the story of how he came to be invisible. Griffin reveals how unhappy and angry he is with the world, and his plan to rule it. He threatens Dr. Kemp with harm unless he agrees to help him.	48
39	**The Escape!**	Griffin learns that Dr. Kemp has tricked him by calling the police. But Griffin gets away. Very angry now, he attacks a man in town, hurting him very badly. Dr. Kemp realizes that, unless he does something very soon, more people will be hurt. He then decides to set a trap for the invisible man.	54
40	**Visible at Last**	Dr. Kemp sets the trap! His idea is to lure Griffin out of his house, and into the town. Once there, the invisible man is trapped. In the end, the man who is determined to bring harm to the world, brings harm upon himself.	60

Comprehension Check Answer Key 67
Vocabulary Check Answer Key 69

WORDS USED

Story 31	Story 32	Story 33	Story 34	Story 35
KEY WORDS				
blind	church	crowd	attack	cheek
bother	peek	disappear	fear	finger
everybody	pretend	escape	helper	poke
fierce	puzzle	loose	mad	polite
scared	robber	stare	notice	speed
skin	scream	touch	slap	teeth
NECESSARY WORDS				
bandage		crazy	dumb	tavern
experiment	haunted	evil	hobo	ouch
hotel	slam	invisible	potion	
stranger	stole/stolen	person	stomach	
temper		wig		
weird				

WORDS USED

Story 36	Story 37	Story 38	Story 39	Story 40
KEY WORDS				
darkness	decide	hate	easily	somehow
forward	foolish	master	fool	struggle
seize	goodness	mirror	intend	through
shake	harm	nobody	safety	trouble
shoot	mistake	spread	since	unless
upstairs	warn	understand	stupid	yet
NECESSARY WORDS				
housecoat		magician	downstairs	choke
		visible		

CTR C-31

THE STRANGE MAN

PREPARATION

Key Words

blind (blīnd) not able to see
  The old man was <u>blind</u> so he couldn't see the traffic.

bother (boTH´ ər) worry; annoy
  The music got so loud that it began to <u>bother</u> Jenny.

everybody (ev´ rē bod´ ē) every person
  <u>Everybody</u> was in the living room, ready to open gifts.

fierce (firs) wild; violent
  The wild dog was so <u>fierce</u>, that even the wolves wouldn't fight him.

scared (skãrd) frightened
  The monster <u>scared</u> the little girl and she ran away.

skin (skin) the outer covering of the body
  Al's <u>skin</u> was covered with bug bites.

THE STRANGE MAN

Necessary Words

bandage (ban´ dij)   a strip of cloth or other material used to cover a wound
> The doctor put a <u>bandage</u> on Judy's cut to keep it from bleeding.

experiment (eks per´ əment)   a trial or test to find out something
> It took many <u>experiments</u> before the space shuttle would fly.

hotel (hō tel´)   a building with many rooms where travelers find rest and food
> John stopped at a nice <u>hotel</u> on his way to New York.

stranger (strān´ gər)   someone not seen or known before
> John is well-known in Colorado, but he feels like a <u>stranger</u> in Kentucky.

temper (tem´ pər)   state of mind
> Mrs. Crabtree has such a bad <u>temper</u>, that she shouts all the time.
>
> Mary has a sweet <u>temper</u>.

weird (wird)   strange; mysterious
> The animal was so <u>weird</u>, that Brian knew he had never seen anything like it before.

People

Mrs. Hall   is the owner of a hotel where the strange man stays. She is a nice person, but very nosy!

CTR C-31

THE STRANGE MAN

Mrs. Hall eyed the stranger as he walked into the hotel. She had never seen such a strange man.

Preview:	1. Read the name of the story.
	2. Look at the picture.
	3. Read the sentences under the picture.
	4. Read the first two paragraphs of the story.
	5. Then answer the following question.

You learned from your preview that
___ a. Mrs. Hall wore big blue glasses.
___ b. the stranger was blind.
___ c. Mrs. Hall was happy to give the stranger a room.
___ d. Mrs. Hall never saw such a strange-looking man.

Turn to the Comprehension Check on page 10 for the right answer.

Now read the story.

Read to find out what Mrs. Hall finds in the stranger's room.

THE STRANGE MAN

Mrs. Hall looked up as the strange man walked in. "I would like to stay in your hotel for a while," he said. Mrs. Hall couldn't answer. She was too surprised. This was the weirdest man she had ever seen.

His face was covered with bandages. He wore gloves and a long coat that went down to his knees. The hat on his head was pulled down low, and he wore big, blue glasses. Mrs. Hall couldn't see his eyes. She thought that he was blind.

"I will pay you well," he said, "but there is one thing. No one must bother me. Everybody must stay away. I have very hard work to do, and if I am bothered, I will not be able to get my experiments done."

"Very well," Mrs. Hall said. The stranger scared her, but she needed the money to help with her bills. He paid her and went to his room.

Soon, everybody in town was talking about the man staying at Mrs. Hall's hotel. They had heard about his fierce temper, and they were all scared of him.

They also tried to guess what was wrong with him. Why did he wear bandages on his face? Some people thought he had burned his skin in a fire. Mrs. Hall told everybody that she had thought he was blind, but she had been wrong. Now she thought he was a doctor, and that was why he couldn't be bothered during his experiments.

One day, a lot of big boxes came for the stranger, and Mrs. Hall had her husband help him carry them. They were filled with many bottles. There were green bottles, blue bottles, red bottles, almost every color you could think of.

"I was right," Mrs. Hall said to herself. "He is a doctor." She wondered if the experiments were safe. Maybe that was how the stranger had gotten hurt. Maybe that's why he had to wear bandages. She wasn't too happy about having him in her hotel.

Mrs. Hall heard barking. She looked and saw the neighbor's dog running at the strange man. "How funny," she thought. "That dog likes everybody, and I have never seen him bark at anyone before."

The strange man yelled at the dog. "Stay away!" he shouted. "Someone get this dog!"

The dog jumped up and bit the strange man on the leg. The stranger shouted fiercely and kicked the dog, and the dog ran away howling.

"I'm sorry he bit you," Mrs. Hall said. "He's never bit anyone before. Are you okay?"

"Yes, I'm fine," the strange man said angrily. "I just want to get these bottles to my room so I can work!"

"What a weird person!" Mrs. Hall thought. She hoped he wasn't hurt. She looked to see where the dog had bitten him to make sure that he was all right.

Mrs. Hall saw the hole in the strange man's pants. Something was wrong, for she couldn't see any skin. She couldn't see anything because the stranger's pant leg was *empty*!

She looked again to make sure, but the strange man had gone back inside the hotel.

"Did I really see that?" she asked herself. Maybe she had been wrong. She would have to keep an eye on her new guest. There was something weird going on indeed!

CTR C-31

THE STRANGE MAN

COMPREHENSION CHECK

Choose the best answer.

> **Preview Answer:**
> d. Mrs. Hall never saw such a strange-looking man.

1. Why did Mrs. Hall think that the stranger was blind?
   ___a. He carried a walking stick.
   ___b. He owned a seeing-eye dog.
   ___c. He was always bumping into things.
   ___d. He wore big, dark glasses and she couldn't see his eyes.

2. What *first* gave Mrs. Hall the idea that the stranger was a doctor?
   ___a. He carried a doctor's bag.
   ___b. He made strange house calls in the middle of the night.
   ___c. He was experimenting in secret.
   ___d. Only a doctor would wear so many bandages.

3. What was it that *convinced* Mrs. Hall that the strange man was a doctor?
   ___a. The many different colored bottles that came for him.
   ___b. He was good at wrapping bandages.
   ___c. He was always at the hospital.
   ___d. He always seemed to work so hard.

4. First, Mrs. Hall heard barking. Then, she saw her neighbor's dog running. Next,
   ___a. the dog took a bite out of Mrs. Hall's arm.
   ___b. the dog jumped up and bit the stranger.
   ___c. Mrs. Hall told the dog to stay away.
   ___d. the stranger kicked the dog.

5. Where did the dog bite the strange man?
   ___a. On his foot
   ___b. On his leg
   ___c. On his arm
   ___d. On his lip

6. Why do you think the dog bit the strange man?
   ___a. He wasn't a friendly dog.
   ___b. He always bit strangers.
   ___c. His owner told him to.
   ___d. He knew there was something evil about the stranger.

7. When Mrs. Hall looked at the hole in the stranger's pants, she saw
   ___a. nothing inside.
   ___b. a bruise.
   ___c. a large, ugly cut.
   ___d. blood.

8. When Mrs. Hall saw the stranger's empty pant leg, she thought
   ___a. he had only one leg.
   ___b. he was playing a trick.
   ___c. she should go home.
   ___d. she was seeing things.

9. Another name for this story could be
   ___a. "A New Man in Town."
   ___b. "The Man with One Leg."
   ___c. "The Strange Doctor."
   ___d. "Mrs. Hall's Hotel."

10. This story is mainly about
    ___a. a strange man in a new town.
    ___b. a man and his experiments.
    ___c. a stranger who likes to wear bandages.
    ___d. a man who likes living in a hotel.

Check your answers with the key on page 67.

This page may be reproduced for classroom use.

CTR C-31

THE STRANGE MAN

VOCABULARY CHECK

| blind | bother | everybody | fierce | scared | skin |

I. Sentences to Finish

Fill in the blank in each sentence with the correct key word from the box above.

1. When Rob showed his _____ temper, his boss fired him.

2. The _____ man takes a long time to cross the street.

3. When I watch the basketball game, I don't want anyone to _____ me.

4. I became _____ when I heard the storm was headed our way.

5. I asked _____ to come to my party on Saturday.

6. Her _____ was cracked and dry from the sun.

II. Crossword Puzzle

Use the key words from the box above to fill in the blanks in the puzzle.

Across

1. frightened
3. not able to see
4. wild or violent

Down

1. outer covering of the body
2. every person
3. to worry or annoy

Check your answers with the key on page 69.

This page may be reproduced for classroom use.

11

CTR C-32

FLYING FURNITURE!

PREPARATION

Key Words

church	(chėrch)	a building where people go to worship God *Every Sunday, Jan and her family go to <u>church</u> and pray.*
peek	(pēk)	look quickly; a quick, sly look *Even though it wasn't her birthday, Sally wanted to <u>peek</u> at her presents.*
pretend	(pri tend´)	make believe *William wanted to <u>pretend</u> he was sick, so he wouldn't have to go to school.*
puzzle	(puz´ l)	confuse; trouble *The strange way that Linda was acting, began to <u>puzzle</u> Fred.* a problem or task to be done for fun *Joe likes to do crossword <u>puzzles</u>.*
robber	(rob´ ər)	thief; person who takes what doesn't belong to him *The police caught the <u>robber</u> as he was breaking into a house.*
scream	(skrēm)	a loud, sharp cry *The movie was so scary, that it made Lisa <u>scream</u>.*

FLYING FURNITURE!

Necessary Words

haunted (´hönted) visited by ghosts
    The <u>haunted</u> house was full of ghosts and witches.

slam (slam) shut with force; close with a 'bang.'
    "Don't <u>slam</u> the door," said Mother, "or it will break."

stole/stolen (stōl) (stō´lən) took something not belonging to you; taken
    John <u>stole</u> the candy from the store; Mother made him bring it back.

    Ann left her bike outside, and it was <u>stolen</u>.

CTR C-32

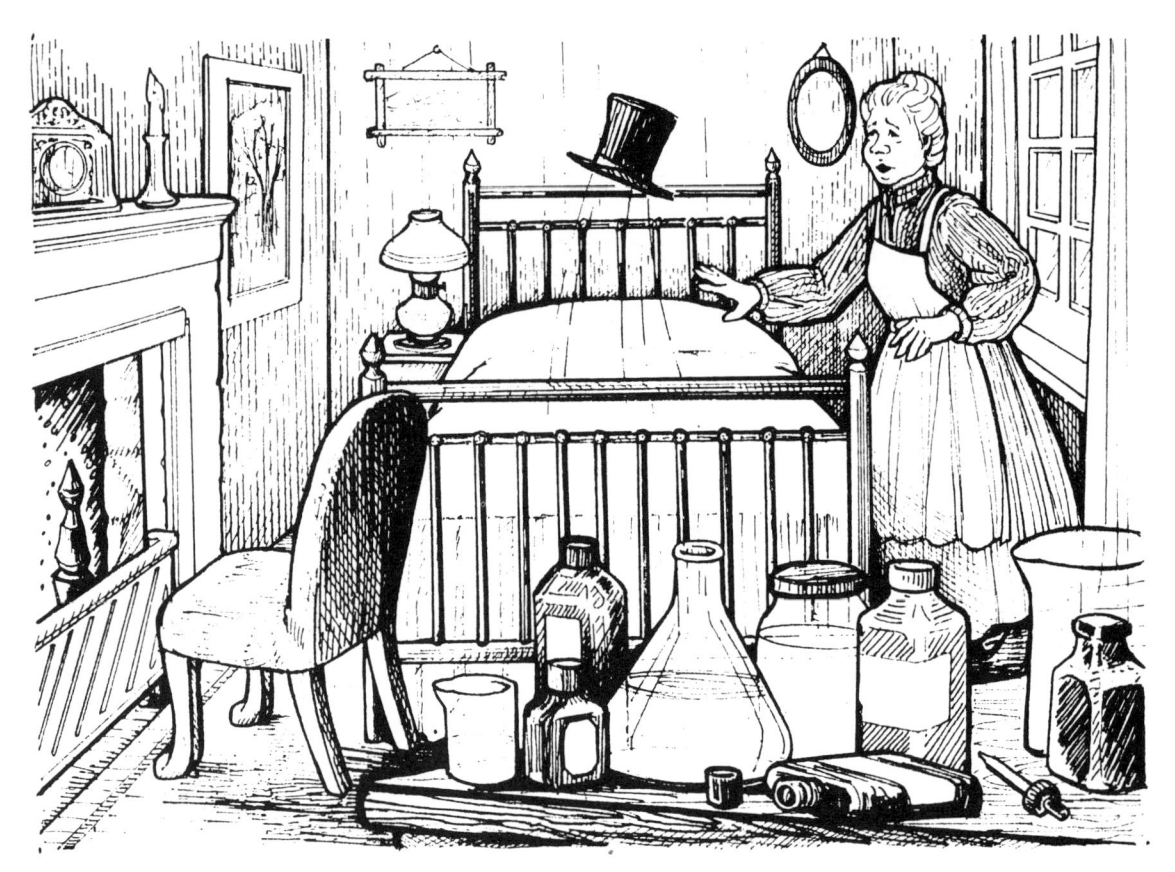

FLYING FURNITURE!

Mrs. Hall's mouth fell open. She wasn't sure if she was seeing things.

Preview: 1. Read the name of the story.
2. Look at the picture.
3. Read the sentences under the picture.
4. Read the first four paragraphs of the story.
5. Then answer the following question.

You learned from your preview that
___ a. Mrs. Hall really liked the strange man.
___ b. the stranger was mean to everybody.
___ c. the stranger liked children.
___ d. the stranger was friendly to dogs.

Turn to the Comprehension Check on page 16 for the right answer.

Now read the story.

Read to find out what happens to Mrs. Hall when she goes to the stranger's room.

14

FLYING FURNITURE!

The strange man stayed at Mrs. Hall's for a long time. He was a puzzle to most of the people in the town. They did not know who he was or what he was doing.

No one in the town liked the stranger. He never spoke to anyone, and he never even smiled at the children. Dogs would only bark at him.

Mrs. Hall tried to pretend that she liked the strange man. She said hello to him everyday, always asking if he needed anything. But the strange man said nothing.

The people of the town began to think he was a terrible man because he was mean to everybody. They were beginning to believe he had done something wrong.

One day, a woman's scream was heard. It came from the town church. When the people got to the church, the woman who had screamed ran out to meet them.

"A robber has just stolen all the money!" she said.

"Did you see the robber?" someone asked.

"No," said the woman. "I heard someone laughing, but I didn't see anyone at all."

Mrs. Hall heard about someone robbing the church, and she was scared. She knew that the strange man had run out of money. She had a feeling that he was the robber.

"What should I do?" Mrs. Hall said to herself. "I wonder if the strange man is here?"

She went to the strange man's room. She was going to pretend that she was cleaning the room. Then she would take a peek and see if she could find the stolen money.

Mrs. Hall slowly opened the door to the strange man's room. It was empty. She stepped inside.

The first thing she did was look on the table. The table was full of glass bottles. There were also papers with many numbers and letters on them. They were puzzling to Mrs. Hall. She guessed it was part of the strange man's experiments.

"I should take a peek at the bed," Mrs. Hall said to herself. "Maybe the strange man hid the money there."

Mrs. Hall went over to the bed. The strange man's hat was in the middle of it. She went to grab the hat.

The hat *moved*!

Mrs. Hall's mouth fell open. She wasn't sure if her eyes had really seen the hat move.

She went to grab the hat again. This time, the hat went straight up in the air. It stayed there and didn't move.

Mrs. Hall was about to scream, when the hat came flying at her. She moved just in time. The hat almost hit her in the face.

Mrs. Hall had never seen anything like this before. It was very, very weird. Maybe the hat was haunted!

The chair next to the strange man's bed began to move. It, too, went straight up in the air. The four legs pointed at Mrs. Hall. Slowly, the chair began to move.

At first, Mrs. Hall couldn't do anything because she was too scared. But when the chair legs touched her, she began to scream.

Mrs. Hall ran out of the room as fast as she could go. She heard the door slam shut behind her. She heard someone laughing, but she did not stop. She wanted to get out of the hotel and find the police.

CTR C-32

FLYING FURNITURE!

COMPREHENSION CHECK

Choose the best answer.

> **Preview Answer:**
> b. the stranger was mean to everybody.

1. The people in town were troubled about the stranger because
   ___a. all the dogs barked at him.
   ___b. he never smiled at them.
   ___c. they didn't know who he was or what he was doing.
   ___d. he wouldn't take off his bandages.

2. Why do you think that Mrs. Hall pretended to like the strange man?
   ___a. She wanted him to ask her out to dinner.
   ___b. She was afraid of him.
   ___c. She was going to ask him for more money for the room.
   ___d. She really wanted to be friends with him.

3. First, a woman's screams were heard. Then, everyone ran to the church. Next,
   ___a. the woman said that she heard someone laughing.
   ___b. the woman said someone had stolen her money.
   ___c. the woman said she didn't really see anyone.
   ___d. the woman told everyone that the church had been robbed.

4. Why did Mrs. Hall think it was the stranger who had robbed the church?
   ___a. He always had a lot of money.
   ___b. He was often seen hanging around the church.
   ___c. She knew the strange man had run out of money.
   ___d. Someone saw him take the money from the church.

5. Mrs. Hall went to the stranger's room to
   ___a. count his bandages.
   ___b. look for the stolen money.
   ___c. look for the rent money.
   ___d. see all the colored bottles.

6. When Mrs. Hall went to the stranger's room, why did she pretend she was cleaning it?
   ___a. She wanted to count all the glass bottles in his room.
   ___b. She wanted the stranger to know that she had cleaned his room.
   ___c. She had nothing else to do.
   ___d. She would have a good reason for being there if the stranger walked in.

7. First, Mrs. Hall went over to the bed. Then, she reached for the stranger's hat. Next,
   ___a. the hat moved.
   ___b. her mouth fell open.
   ___c. the hat went straight up in the air.
   ___d. Mrs. Hall screamed.

8. Mrs. Hall screamed when
   ___a. the chair began to move.
   ___b. the hat almost hit her in the face.
   ___c. the door slammed shut.
   ___d. the chair legs touched her.

9. Another name for this story could be
   ___a. "Stolen Money."
   ___b. "The Haunted House."
   ___c. "Strange Happenings."
   ___d. "Nosey Mrs. Hall."

10. This story is mainly about
    ___a. a strange man's experiments.
    ___b. a church that was robbed.
    ___c. a haunted hat.
    ___d. the strange events that have taken place since the stranger arrived in town.

Check your answers with the key on page 67.

This page may be reproduced for classroom use.

CTR C-32

FLYING FURNITURE!

VOCABULARY CHECK

| church | peek | pretend | puzzle | robber | scream |

I. Sentences to Finish

Fill in the blank in each sentence with the correct key word from the box above.

1. When the police arrived at the bank, the _____ ran away.

2. On Sunday, the _____ will have a picnic.

3. It was a _____ as to how I was locked out of the house.

4. When my sister took my best sweater, I wanted to _____ .

5. Sometimes I _____ that I am a rock star.

6. Before going to bed, I sometimes _____ in the closet first.

II. Mixed-Up Words

First, unscramble the key words in COLUMN A. Then, draw a line to its meaning in COLUMN B.

A.		B.
1. acrems _____		a. a building where people go to worship God
2. rebrob _____		b. look quickly; a sly look
3. tenderp _____		c. confuse; trouble
4. keep _____		d. thief
5. rucchh _____		e. a loud, sharp cry
6. lezzup _____		f. make believe

Check your answers with the key on page 69.

This page may be reproduced for classroom use.

CTR C-33

INVISIBLE!

PREPARATION

Key Words

crowd (kroud)   a large number of people together
There was at least one hundred people in the <u>crowd</u>.

disappear (dis´ ə pir´)   pass from sight
The magician made the rabbit <u>disappear</u> into thin air.

escape (es kāp´)   get free
"Your secret will never <u>escape</u> my lips," said Sally to her friend.

loose (lüs)   not tight
Albert tightened the <u>loose</u> screw so it wouldn't fall off.
free
I tried to hold on to the thief, but he broke <u>loose</u>.

stare (stãr)   a fixed look with eyes wide open
Mary thought the boy was so cute, that she couldn't help but <u>stare</u> at him.

touch (tuch)   feel
The cat looked very soft, making Ann want to <u>touch</u> it.

INVISIBLE!

Necessary Words

crazy (krā´ zē)   not of sound mind
The crowd thought Jim was crazy when he said he would eat a whole watermelon.

evil (ē´ vl)   very bad; wicked
The evil wizard turned the princess into a monkey.

invisible (in viz´ ə bl)   not able to be seen
Bill wished he was invisible so his mother couldn't find him.

person (pėr´ sn)   man, woman or child
Bob is a nice person and I like him very much.

wig (wig)   a covering of hair for the head
Mr. Jones wore a wig to cover his bald head.

CTR C-33

INVISIBLE!

The strange man had no face! He had no head! He had no hands!

> ***Preview:***   1. Read the name of the story.
> 2. Look at the picture.
> 3. Read the sentences under the picture.
> 4. Read the first five paragraphs of the story.
> 5. Then answer the following question.
>
> You learned from your preview that
> ___ a. the crowd thought that Mrs. Hall was crazy.
> ___ b. the stranger was the robber who stole from the church.
> ___ c. Mrs. Hall's clothes were haunted.
> ___ d. there was nothing evil in the strange man's room.
>
> *Turn to the Comprehension Check on page 22 for the right answer.*

Now read the story.

Read to find out just how strange this man really is.

20

INVISIBLE!

Mrs. Hall screamed all the way down the stairs. When everybody heard her scream, they came to see what was going on. Soon, Mrs. Hall had a crowd at her hotel door.

"What is wrong?" a policeman asked Mrs. Hall.

"There's something evil in the strange man's room! His clothes are *haunted*!"

The crowd began to stare at Mrs. Hall. They thought she was crazy. No one knew what she was talking about.

"It's true!" she said. "I went up to his room. I thought that he was the robber who stole from the church. I went to look under his hat . . . and it moved!"

"Are you sure?" the policeman asked.

"Yes! His hat flew at my face. Then his chair went up in the air and it pushed me out of his room!"

"Well, where is this person?" asked the policeman. "I would like to talk with him."

"I don't know," answered Mrs. Hall. "I haven't seen him all day."

"Let's look in his room," the policeman said. The crowd moved into Mrs. Hall's hotel.

They found the stranger standing by the stairs. He didn't say a word as the crowd came up to him.

"See here!" Mrs. Hall said. "Where have you been? The church was just robbed, and no one has seen you. Strange things have happened in your room. I want to know what's going on, or you'll have to leave my hotel!"

The crowd was silent. They all stared, waiting for the strange man to speak.

The stranger laughed. Finally, he spoke. "I'll show you what's going on."

He began to pull on his nose. The crowd could not believe what they were seeing. The strange man's nose seemed to be loose.

"Here," he said to Mrs. Hall. "Catch!"

Mrs. Hall looked up as the strange man's nose dropped into her hand. It wasn't real!

Then the strange man took off his gloves. Mrs. Hall's eyes grew very big. The strange man had no hands!

Next, he grabbed his hair and threw it up in the air. His hair was a wig. He began to take off the bandages from his face. When he was done, the crowd could not believe it!

The strange man had no face! He had no head! He had no hands!

"Oh my!" Mrs. Hall said. "He's . . . he's invisible. He's an invisible man!"

"That's right," said the invisible man. He began to take off the rest of his clothes as fast as he could.

"Don't let him take off his clothes," the policeman shouted. "He'll disappear, and we won't be able to see him. He'll escape!"

The crowd jumped at the invisible man. Some didn't want to touch him. One policeman grabbed him. He could feel the invisible man's hand, but he couldn't see it.

"Don't let him loose. It's okay to touch him. Grab on tight!"

But it was too late. The invisible man had taken off all his clothes. He had pulled away from the policeman and had disappeared. The crowd heard him laugh as he ran away.

"Oh no!" cried Mrs. Hall. "What are we going to do now? If we can't see him, we'll never find him. The invisible man has escaped!"

CTR C-33

INVISIBLE!

COMPREHENSION CHECK

Choose the best answer.

Preview Answer:
a. the crowd thought that Mrs. Hall was crazy.

1. First, Mrs. Hall screamed all the way down the stairs. Then, a crowd gathered at her hotel. Next,
   ___a. she asked someone to call the police.
   ___b. she told the crowd she had seen something evil.
   ___c. she told the crowd that the stranger's clothes were haunted.
   ___d. she found the robber.

2. The crowd thought that Mrs. Hall was crazy because
   ___a. they didn't know what she was talking about.
   ___b. she couldn't stop screaming.
   ___c. she stared at the crowd.
   ___d. she said there was something evil in the church.

3. When the crowd moved into the hotel, they found the stranger standing by the stairs. He
   ___a. told the crowd that, yes, he had robbed the church.
   ___b. didn't say a word.
   ___c. laughed at everyone.
   ___d. said he was going to leave the hotel.

4. When the stranger pulled off his nose, he
   ___a. threw it in the air.
   ___b. dropped it on the floor.
   ___c. told a policeman to catch it.
   ___d. he threw it to Mrs. Hall.

5. When the crowd discovered that the stranger had no hands,
   ___a. they ran from the hotel.
   ___b. they pulled on his wig.
   ___c. they tried to pull his bandages off.
   ___d. they could not believe it!

6. Why did the invisible man undress so quickly?
   ___a. So he would not be seen and he could escape.
   ___b. Mrs. Hall asked him to.
   ___c. He wanted to put on a new set of clothes.
   ___d. He had to go somewhere else in a hurry.

7. The crowd jumped at the invisible man but
   ___a. only one policeman grabbed him.
   ___b. only one person could feel him.
   ___c. some people did not want to touch him.
   ___d. Mrs. Hall tried to help him get away.

8. Why did the invisible man laugh as he ran away?
   ___a. Because when he was scared, he always laughed.
   ___b. He scared everyone and got away with it.
   ___c. He heard someone tell a funny joke.
   ___d. Someone had tickled him.

9. Another name for this story could be
   ___a. "Now You See Me, Now You Don't."
   ___b. "The Stranger Who Liked to Laugh."
   ___c. "The Man Who Wouldn't Wear Clothes."
   ___d. "Another Day at the Hotel."

10. This story is mainly about
    ___a. a woman and her haunted hotel.
    ___b. an evil man who brings fear wherever he goes.
    ___c. an evil man who liked to laugh.
    ___d. a man who liked to undress himself.

Check your answers with the key on page 67.

This page may be reproduced for classroom use.

CTR C-33

INVISIBLE!

VOCABULARY CHECK

| crowd | disappear | escape | loose | stare | touch |

I. Sentences to Finish

Fill in the blank in each sentence with the correct key word from the box above.

1. My tooth was _____ , so Mother took me to the dentist.

2. The robber was locked in the jail so he wouldn't _____ .

3. When a store has a big sale, they are sure to attract a large _____ .

4. The cookies seem to _____ as fast as Mother makes them.

5. When I _____ in the mirror, I like what I see.

6. The teacher told us to look at, but not _____ , the snake.

II. True or False

Are the key words used correctly? Check YES or NO.

	YES	NO
1. If there is a <u>crowd</u>, there are many people.	___	___
2. If something <u>disappears</u>, it can be seen.	___	___
3. A <u>loose</u> wheel will help me win the car race.	___	___
4. If I <u>escape</u>, it means that I am free.	___	___
5. Henry will <u>stare</u> at the cheese and it will melt.	___	___
6. If you <u>touch</u> the chair, it means that you like it.	___	___

Check your answers with the key on page 69.

This page may be reproduced for classroom use.

CTR C-34

THE UNHAPPY HELPER

PREPARATION

Key Words

attack	(ə tak´)	go against an enemy; set upon to hurt *The army began to <u>attack</u> the town with tanks.*
fear	(fir)	a feeling that danger or evil is near; feel afraid of *The bully was so mean, that Greg lived in <u>fear</u> of seeing him.* *I will not <u>fear</u> that mean boy just because he is tall.*
helper	(help´ər)	a person who helps *Mr. Smith asked his <u>helper</u> to clean the schoolyard.*
mad	(mad)	angry *After he called her fat, Jane was <u>mad</u> at Ralph.*
notice	(nō´ tis)	pay attention to; see *Wally didn't <u>notice</u> the "No Swimming" sign until he was in the pool.*
slap	(´slap)	hit with an open hand *The woman wanted to <u>slap</u> the man across the face with her hand.*

THE UNHAPPY HELPER

Necessary Words

dumb (dum) stupid
Linda felt <u>dumb</u> when she gave the wrong answer to the question.

hobo (hō bō) tramp; a man who wanders about and begs
The <u>hobo</u> had holes in his shoes and wore dirty clothes.

potion (pō sh n) magic drink
Richard drank the love <u>potion</u> without knowing it.

stomach (stum k) a part of the body containing the stomach
After eating so much candy, Dave had a <u>stomach</u> ache.

People

Mr. Marvel is a hobo who lives next to the town. It is an unlucky day for him when he meets the invisible man!

CTR C-34

THE UNHAPPY HELPER

"I want you to help me," a voice said.

> **Preview:**
> 1. Read the name of the story.
> 2. Look at the picture.
> 3. Read the sentence under the picture.
> 4. Read the first five paragraphs of the story.
> 5. Then answer the following question.
>
> You learned from your preview that
> ___ a. Mr. Marvel liked to sleep.
> ___ b. Mr. Marvel was a man who worried a lot.
> ___ c. Mr. Marvel was a nice man who liked to be left alone.
> ___ d. Mr. Marvel was always hearing strange noises.
>
> *Turn to the Comprehension Check on page 28 for the right answer.*

Now read the story.

Read to find out how Mr. Marvel came to be the invisible man's helper.

26

THE UNHAPPY HELPER

Mr. Marvel was a hobo who lived close to town. He was a nice man who liked to be left alone. He didn't want to hurt anyone, and he didn't want anyone to hurt him.

Mr. Marvel was sleeping under a tree, next to where he lived, when he heard a sound. He wasn't sure what the sound was, but it sounded like someone running.

He looked behind him. He didn't notice anything, so he went back to sleeping.

"I want you to help me," a voice said.

Mr. Marvel looked again. He still noticed nothing. There was no one there. Was he hearing things? Mr. Marvel began to worry.

"You can't see me," the voice said. "But I can see you. I am an invisible man."

Mr. Marvel laughed. "There is no such thing as an invisible man, so come out from where you are hiding!"

"Don't make me mad," the voice said, "or I will hurt you. I want you to be my helper. If you don't help me, you'll be sorry."

"Ha!" said Mr. Marvel. "Why should I fear something I can't see?"

Then, all of a sudden, Mr. Marvel felt a hard slap across his face. Then something hit him in the stomach and knocked him down.

"I will teach you to fear me," the voice said. "You will be my helper from now on, and you will do what I say. If you don't, I'll do away with you. You can't see me, so you will never know where I am. I can hurt you anytime I want. Don't make me mad again. Got it?"

Mr. Marvel got another slap across his face. He knew he would have to be the invisible man's helper. He was very scared.

The invisible man made Mr. Marvel go into town. He wanted Mr. Marvel to get the papers he had left in Mrs. Hall's hotel. The invisible man needed those papers to make the potion that made him disappear.

"Don't be dumb," the invisible man told Mr. Marvel. "I'll be watching always, and I can attack at any time."

Mr. Marvel walked into Mrs. Hall's hotel. He was really scared now. He feared the invisible man very much. No one in the hotel noticed Mr. Marvel. He went to the invisible man's room and got the papers.

On the way out the door, a policeman noticed Mr. Marvel.

"What have you got there?" the policeman asked him.

"Nothing," Mr. Marvel said. He knew the invisible man was watching him.

"What are those papers in your hand?" the policeman asked.

Suddenly, the policeman hit the ground. He began to shout.

"Help! Help!" the policeman cried. "I'm under attack! The invisible man is kicking me!"

The town went wild. People were running everywhere. Everyone was screaming because the invisible man kept hitting people and hurting them. No one could see him. They couldn't catch him. But they heard his evil laugh.

Mr. Marvel ran out of the town as fast as he could go. He wanted to get away from the invisible man. But he wasn't fast enough. The invisible man caught him.

"You aren't going anywhere," the invisible man said. "You will do what I say."

"I don't want to be your helper," Mr. Marvel said. "You are mean to hurt people."

"That's right. And I'll hurt you if you ever try to run away again."

The invisible man pushed Mr. Marvel to the ground. He took the papers out of Mr. Marvel's hand.

"Get moving," the invisible man told him.

So poor Mr. Marvel started walking. He feared for his life. The invisible man was everywhere. There was nothing Mr. Marvel could do.

CTR C-34

THE UNHAPPY HELPER

COMPREHENSION CHECK

Choose the best answer.

> **Preview Answer:**
> c. Mr. Marvel was a nice man who liked to be left alone.

1. Mr. Marvel was
   ___a. a clean, nice man.
   ___b. a friendly hobo who lived in town.
   ___c. a hobo who didn't like to be left alone.
   ___d. a hobo who lived in a tree.

2. Mr. Marvel awoke from sleep when he thought he heard
   ___a. someone shouting.
   ___b. someone running.
   ___c. a strange sound.
   ___d. the ice cream man.

3. Mr. Marvel laughed when
   ___a. he thought he was hearing things.
   ___b. he thought he was having a bad dream.
   ___c. he knew what the voice was.
   ___d. he was told that the voice was really an invisible man.

4. First, Mr. Marvel felt a hard slap across his face. Then,
   ___a. something hit him in the stomach.
   ___b. something knocked him down.
   ___c. a voice told him that he would not make a good helper.
   ___d. something knocked his house down.

5. Mr. Marvel became scared when
   ___a. he had to go into town.
   ___b. he knew that there really was an invisible man.
   ___c. something pulled on his hair.
   ___d. he was hit in the stomach again.

6. Why was Mr. Marvel sent to Mrs. Hall's hotel?
   ___a. To steal some newspapers from the stranger's room
   ___b. To pay the stranger's rent
   ___c. To get a policeman
   ___d. To get some very important papers for the invisible man

7. How did the policeman know that he was being attacked by an invisible man?
   ___a. He was being beat up by someone he could not see.
   ___b. Mr. Marvel told him so.
   ___c. His attacker wore a name plate.
   ___d. He could hear someone laughing.

8. The town went "wild" because
   ___a. Mr. Marvel ran out of the town.
   ___b. they couldn't catch him fast enough.
   ___c. the invisible man was hurting everyone.
   ___d. Mr. Marvel was laughing.

9. Another name for this story could be
   ___a. "The Stranger and His New Friend."
   ___b. "The Scary Hobo."
   ___c. "The Invisible Man Finds a Helper."
   ___d. "The Town Makes Friends with a Stranger."

10. This story is mainly about
    ___a. a very scared hobo.
    ___b. the invisible man hurting everyone.
    ___c. Mr. Marvel finding trouble.
    ___d. a nice man who is forced to help a mean person.

Check your answers with the key on page 67.

This page may be reproduced for classroom use.

CTR C-34

THE UNHAPPY HELPER

VOCABULARY CHECK

| attack | fear | helper | mad | notice | slap |

I. Sentences to Finish

Fill in the blank in each sentence with the correct key word from the box above.

1. It makes me _____ when I forget to bring my lunch to school.

2. I was happy when my brother didn't _____ that I took his bike.

3. If someone were to _____ me, I would hit back.

4. My dog has a terrible _____ of storms.

5. A cat will _____ a bird if you leave them alone together.

6. Father was looking for a _____ to help him rake the yard.

II. Word Search

Find the key words in the puzzle below. They may be written from left to right or from top to bottom. Circle each one. One word, that is not a key word, has been done for you.

```
Z  U  H  M  A  D  V  R  S
O  T  E  W  N  S  P  Q  L
Q  B  L  E  D  B  Z  X  A
G  H  P  F  O  X  F  T  P
A  F  E  N  O  T  I  C  E
V  E  R  X  N  Z  A  V  X
L  A  T  T  A  C  K  L  T
S  R  P  W  X  Y (A  N  Y)
```

Check your answers with the key on page 70.

This page may be reproduced for classroom use.

MORE FEAR IN A NEW TOWN

PREPARATION

Key Words

cheek	(chēk)	side of the face below either eye *His grandmother pinched his <u>cheek</u> for being bad.*
finger	(fing´ gər)	one of the five members found on the hand *The teacher showed Alice where to put each <u>finger</u> on the piano keys.*
poke	(pōk)	push against with something pointed, like a finger *The farmer tried to <u>poke</u> the seed into the ground.*
polite	(pə līt)	showing good manners *Carol knew it wasn't <u>polite</u> to wipe her shoes on the carpet.*
speed	(spēd)	go fast *The driver started to <u>speed</u>, and passed the slower truck.*
teeth	(tēth)	more than one tooth *The dentist told Shirley to brush her <u>teeth</u> twice a day.*

MORE FEAR IN A NEW TOWN

Necessary Words

ouch   (ouch)   a sound a person makes to express sudden pain
                                                 "Ouch!" said Tom, as the mosquito bit him.

tavern   (tav´ərn)   place where alcoholic drinks are served; saloon
                                                 The men went to the tavern to have something to drink.

CTR C-35

MORE FEAR IN A NEW TOWN

"Help somebody! Something very strange is going on in the tavern!"

Preview: 1. Read the name of the story.
2. Look at the picture.
3. Read the sentences under the picture.
4. Read the first four paragraphs of the story.
5. Then answer the following question.

You learned from your preview that
___ a. Mr. Marvel wanted to hurt the invisible man.
___ b. Mr. Marvel liked to take long walks.
___ c. Mr. Marvel lived in great fear.
___ d. Mr. Marvel liked to sleep.

Turn to the Comprehension Check on page 34 for the right answer.

Now read the story.

Read to find out what the invisible man is up to next.

MORE FEAR IN A NEW TOWN

Mr. Marvel didn't like this new life at all. The invisible man made him walk for hours and hours without a rest. Mr. Marvel's feet began to hurt him very much.

When they would finally stop to rest, Mr. Marvel couldn't get any sleep. He couldn't stop thinking about the invisible man. He could not see him, but he could always hear him.

"Don't you think about trying to escape," the invisible man would say. "You know what will happen." Then he would poke Mr. Marvel in the cheek with his finger.

Sometimes the invisible man would slap him. Mr. Marvel lived in fear. He never knew if the invisible man would hurt him or not.

They were walking to another town. As they got closer to the town, a man on a horse rode up to them.

"Don't tell him about me," the invisible man whispered in Mr. Marvel's ear. "Or else!" The invisible man pulled hard on Mr. Marvel's cheek.

"*Ouch!*" Mr. Marvel said.

The man on the horse looked puzzled. He stared at Mr. Marvel.

"Why did you just say ouch?" the man on the horse asked him.

Mr. Marvel had to think of something quick. "I said ouch because... I have bad teeth," Mr. Marvel said, "and they are hurting me."

"Oh," said the man on the horse. "I know a person in town who can take care of your teeth." The man gave Mr. Marvel another strange look, then rode away at great speed.

"That was very good," the invisible man said to Mr. Marvel. He poked Mr. Marvel in the stomach. "You better be smart like that all the time."

When they got into the new town, the invisible man told Mr. Marvel to stay right in the center of town and not move. Mr. Marvel did as he was told. He didn't want to get hurt anymore.

A sailor came up to Mr. Marvel. "Hello," said the sailor. He pointed his finger at Mr. Marvel. "Do you live here?"

Mr. Marvel didn't want to talk to the sailor. He was afraid that the invisible man would get mad.

"No," Mr. Marvel answered. He didn't have time to be polite. He turned his back to the sailor.

But the sailor didn't go away. He kept right on talking.

"Did you hear what was going on in the town next to this one?" the sailor asked. "There's talk of an invisible man that attacked the town!"

Mr. Marvel didn't know what to say. He wished the sailor would leave.

"No, I didn't hear anything," Mr. Marvel said as politely as he could to the sailor. "I don't talk much."

There was shouting from the tavern next to Mr. Marvel. A man ran out into the street.

"Help, somebody! Something very strange is going on in the tavern!"

"Is someone robbing it?" the sailor asked.

"No," the man said, looking puzzled. "But the money is... just floating away by itself!"

Mr. Marvel could take no more. He turned and began to run with great speed. He just had to get away.

He heard the invisible man behind him. He knew that it would take all the speed he had to keep the invisible man from catching him. If the invisible man did catch him...

As he ran through the town, Mr. Marvel began to shout. Everybody heard Mr. Marvel shouting. When they heard what he was saying, they went inside their houses and locked the doors. They heard two people running, but they saw only one.

And Mr. Marvel kept shouting: "THE INVISIBLE MAN IS COMING! THE INVISIBLE MAN!"

CTR C-35

MORE FEAR IN A NEW TOWN

COMPREHENSION CHECK

Choose the best answer.

> **Preview Answer:**
> c. Mr. Marvel lived in great fear.

1. Mr. Marvel didn't like his new life at all because
   ___a. he couldn't see the invisible man.
   ___b. he was made to live in fear.
   ___c. he never got enough sleep.
   ___d. his feet always hurt.

2. Why did Mr. Marvel tell the man on the horse that he had bad teeth?
   ___a. Because his tooth was loose
   ___b. Because he had said, "Ouch!"
   ___c. Because he had to think of something quick
   ___d. Because it was a reason to explain why he was talking to himself

3. When the invisible man told Mr. Marvel to stand in the center of town and not move, why didn't Mr. Marvel run away?
   ___a. He was afraid of getting hurt again.
   ___b. He was too busy talking to a sailor.
   ___c. He couldn't run anymore because his feet hurt.
   ___d. He was too cold to run.

4. First, a sailor spoke to Mr. Marvel. Mr. Marvel turned his back to the sailor. Then,
   ___a. the sailor kept right on talking.
   ___b. the sailor asked him if he was feeling well.
   ___c. the sailor asked him why he wasn't being polite.
   ___d. the sailor asked him why he was wearing such old clothes.

5. What strange thing was going on in the tavern?
   ___a. Bottles were floating in the air.
   ___b. Everybody in the tavern was screaming.
   ___c. Money was floating away by itself.
   ___d. Money and bottles were floating in the air.

6. The money was floating away by itself because
   ___a. a breeze came through the window and blew it around the tavern.
   ___b. a man in the tavern was throwing money everywhere.
   ___c. the invisible man was stealing it.
   ___d. someone in the tavern left the fan on.

7. Mr. Marvel could take no more. He had to get away. He ran
   ___a. through the town with great speed.
   ___b. to the tavern for a drink.
   ___c. back to his home to rest under a tree.
   ___d. back to Mrs. Hall's hotel.

8. As he ran through the town, Mr. Marvel kept shouting,
   ___a. "The invisible man is coming. The invisible man!"
   ___b. "Help me! He's going to get me."
   ___c. "The invisible man just robbed the tavern!"
   ___d. "Everyone lock your doors. The invisible man is here!"

9. Another name for this story could be
   ___a. "The Haunted Tavern."
   ___b. "The Invisble Man Strikes Again."
   ___c. "Strange Face . . . Strange Place."
   ___d. "Mr. Marvel and the Sailor."

10. This story is mainly about
    ___a. an invisible man who likes to travel.
    ___b. an invisible man who robs taverns.
    ___c. an invisible man who doesn't like hobos.
    ___d. an evil man who fears no one.

Check your answers with the key on page 67.

This page may be reproduced for classroom use.

34

MORE FEAR IN A NEW TOWN

VOCABULARY CHECK

| cheek | finger | poke | polite | speed | teeth |

I. Sentences to Finish

Fill in the blank in each sentence with the correct key word from the box above.

1. My baby brother tried to _____ the cat, but it ran away.

2. The ball hit me in the _____ , just below my left eye.

3. John let out a scream when the window slammed down on his _____ .

4. It is _____ to say 'please' and 'thank you.'

5. Jan's _____ were white from brushing them often.

6. The car raced by with such _____ , that I didn't see its color.

II. Put an X next to the best ending for each sentence.

1. To be <u>polite</u>
   _____ a. is to smile at someone.
   _____ b. is to show good manners.

2. To <u>speed</u>
   _____ a. is to take one's time getting somewhere.
   _____ b. is to go very fast.

3. To <u>poke</u>
   _____ a. is to push against with something pointed.
   _____ b. is to pull something with all your might.

4. A <u>finger</u>
   _____ a. is used to brush your teeth.
   _____ b. can be found on your hand.

5. A <u>cheek</u>
   _____ a. can be found below the eye.
   _____ b. can be found below the bottom lip.

6. Teeth
   _____ a. make all foods taste good.
   _____ b. help you to chew your food.

Check your answers with the key on page 70.

This page may be reproduced for classroom use.

CTR C-36

DR. KEMP'S VISITOR

PREPARATION

Key Words

darkness	(därk´nis)	lack of light; being dark *Once the lights were out, <u>darkness</u> filled the house.*
forward	(fôr´wərd)	ahead; to the front *Roger kept moving <u>forward</u> to get out of the forest.*
seize	(sēz)	take hold of suddenly; grasp *The police wanted to <u>seize</u> the crooks before they stole again.*
shake	(shāk)	move quickly backward or forward, up and down, or from side to side *Jill told Phil to <u>shake</u> the juice before he drank it.*
shoot	(shüt)	hit with a bullet or arrow; fire (a gun, etc.) *I was told to <u>shoot</u> the spot with the arrow.*
upstairs	(up´stãrz´)	up the stairs; on an upper floor *Grandma was too old to keep going <u>upstairs</u>, so we moved her bedroom to the first floor.*

CTR C-36

DR. KEMP'S VISITOR

Necessary Words

housecoat   (hau´ skōt)   a robe-like garment for wear around the house
"Before Mother went shopping, she took off her <u>housecoat</u> and put on a dress.

People

Dr. Kemp   is the doctor who gets a surprise visit from an "old friend."

CTR C-36

DR. KEMP'S VISITOR

"I know you, Kemp," the voice said. "And you know me."

> ***Preview:***
> 1. Read the name of the story.
> 2. Look at the picture.
> 3. Read the sentences under the picture.
> 4. Read the first three paragraphs of the story.
> 5. Then answer the following question.
>
> You learned from your preview that Mr. Marvel
> ___ a. was tired of running and so he gave up.
> ___ b. knew if he could make it to the tavern, he might be safe.
> ___ c. knew that he could outrun the invisible man.
> ___ d. went to the tavern for a drink.
>
> *Turn to the Comprehension Check on page 40 for the right answer.*

Now read the story.

Read to find out about the invisible man's new helper.

DR. KEMP'S VISITOR

Mr. Marvel knew that soon the invisible man would catch him. He could not run fast enough. He heard the invisible man right in back of him.

"I can't give up," Mr. Marvel said to himself. "I can't let him get me. If I do, the invisible man will kill me."

Mr. Marvel noticed a tavern up the road. If he could just make it to the tavern, then he might be safe. He ran to the tavern as fast as he could.

He reached the door. "Open up! Please open up!" Mr. Marvel shouted. "The invisible man is right behind me! He'll kill me if you don't help."

Marvel fell forward into the tavern. He was so scared, he began to shake.

There were two men inside the tavern. One of them had a gun. When Mr. Marvel fell inside, they shut the tavern door.

"What's this about the invisible man?" said the man with the gun. "Where is he?"

"He's right behind me," said Mr. Marvel. "He's going to try and hurt me. I won't be his helper anymore. Shoot him!"

"Don't worry," said the man with the gun. "When he comes in the door, I'll stop him with my gun. Then we will seize him."

"How?" said the other man in the tavern. "We won't be able to see him."

Before the man could answer, the window next to the door broke open.

"It's him!" said Mr. Marvel. "It's the invisible man!"

The man with the gun waited. He couldn't shoot the invisible man because he couldn't see him. The man with the gun took a step forward, holding his gun very tightly.

"I know he's in here," Mr. Marvel said. "I can tell. Please help me! Don't let him get me."

The man with the gun saw the chair next to Mr. Marvel, move.

"Watch out!" shouted the man with the gun. "There he is!" He fired at the spot where the chair had moved. He heard a scream. Then, the chair flew across the room and broke the light. The tavern was now in darkness.

"No one move!" said the man with the gun. "He's knocked out the light with the chair. I think I got him."

There was no sound. They could see nothing in the darkness. Then, the front door opened and they heard someone running away. The invisible man was gone.

***

Dr. Kemp was a friendly doctor who lived close to the tavern. He heard the shot fired. He hoped that nothing bad was going on.

He went back to reading his paper when, suddenly, he heard a noise upstairs in his house. It sounded like glass breaking.

Dr. Kemp went upstairs very quietly, thinking a robber was in his house. He went into every room upstairs, but he saw nothing.

He was about to go back down the stairs, when he noticed something strange. It looked like a spot on the carpet. He touched it with his finger. It was wet, but he couldn't tell what it was. But, for sure, it wasn't water!

"Help me," a voice said. "That's my blood."

Dr. Kemp looked around, but he didn't see anyone. Was this a trick?

"Please, Kemp, you must help me," the voice said again. "I've been shot."

"Who are you?" Dr. Kemp asked. "Where are you? And how do you know my name?"

Just then, Dr. Kemp saw his own housecoat moving down the hall. It was just hanging in the air! Dr. Kemp couldn't believe his eyes!

"I know you, Kemp," the voice said. "And you know me."

Dr. Kemp felt hands seize him and shake him, but he could still see no one there.

"I am the invisible man," the voice said. "I've been shot. You must help me, Kemp, or I will die!"

CTR C-36

DR. KEMP'S VISITOR

COMPREHENSION CHECK

Choose the best answer.

Preview Answer:
b. knew if he could make it to the tavern, he might be safe.

1. Mr. Marvel ran, knowing that the invisible man would soon catch him because
   - ___a. the invisible man always knew where to find him.
   - ___b. he could not run fast enough.
   - ___c. he ran the wrong way.
   - ___d. he decided to give up.

2. Mr. Marvel ran to a tavern. Inside, he found
   - ___a. a large crowd.
   - ___b. three men.
   - ___c. no one.
   - ___d. two men.

3. One of the men in the tavern had
   - ___a. a gun.
   - ___b. a knife.
   - ___c. a club.
   - ___d. a big stick.

4. The invisible man broke into the tavern through a window. Why didn't he use the door?
   - ___a. He wanted to frighten everyone by breaking the glass.
   - ___b. He knew that anyone inside would be waiting for him at the door.
   - ___c. He liked to climb through windows.
   - ___d. The door was locked.

5. First, the window next to the door broke open. Then, the man with the gun waited. He fired his gun when
   - ___a. the invisible man stepped forward.
   - ___b. he saw the chair move.
   - ___c. Mr. Marvel got out of the way.
   - ___d. he heard someone scream.

6. Dr. Kemp
   - ___a. was a friendly doctor who lived close to the tavern.
   - ___b. was a friendly doctor who liked to read the paper.
   - ___c. was a friendly doctor who lived in the tavern.
   - ___d. was a friendly robber.

7. Dr. Kemp checked the rooms upstairs when he heard
   - ___a. someone walking around.
   - ___b. a robber in the house.
   - ___c. a window slam shut.
   - ___d. glass breaking.

8. Dr. Kemp couldn't believe his eyes when
   - ___a. he heard a voice call his name.
   - ___b. he saw his housecoat moving down the hall.
   - ___c. he felt something seize him.
   - ___d. a voice told him that he would die.

9. Another name for this story could be
   - ___a. "A Voice in the Dark."
   - ___b. "A Shooting in the Tavern."
   - ___c. "The Invisible Man Seeks Help."
   - ___d. "A Tavern in Darkness."

10. This story is mainly about
    - ___a. a hobo who finds freedom.
    - ___b. a hobo who brings fear to a town.
    - ___c. an invisible man who likes to break windows.
    - ___d. an evil man who looks for someone to help him stay alive.

Check your answers with the key on page 67.

This page may be reproduced for classroom use.

CTR C-36

DR. KEMP'S VISITOR

VOCABULARY CHECK

| darkness | forward | seize | shake | shoot | upstairs |

I. Sentences to Finish

Choose two key words from the box above to complete the following sentences. Each key word is used twice.

1. John took a step _____ in the _____ and tripped over the toy.

2. When the thief aimed his gun to _____ the man, the man's dog jumped up to _____ him.

3. When the robber found me _____ in my bedroom, I began to _____ .

4. In my bedroom _____ , I sometimes feel all alone in the _____ .

5. Father jumped _____ to _____ the gun from the robber.

6. If my hands were to _____ , I couldn't _____ the arrow straight.

II. Matching

Unscramble the group of letters to spell out the key words. Match the key words in Column A with their meanings in Column B.

COLUMN A   COLUMN B

kehas   1. _____   a. lack of light, being dark

arrofdw   2. _____   b. hit with a bullet or arrow; fire

strupias   3. _____   c. move quickly backward or forward, up and down, or from side to side

sneakdrs   4. _____   d. up the stairs; on an upper floor

thoso   5. _____   e. take hold of suddenly; grasp

esize   6. _____   f. ahead, to the front

Check your answers with the key on page 70.

This page may be reproduced for classroom use.

CTR C-37

FRIEND OR ENEMY?

PREPARATION

Key Words

decide	(di sīd´)	make up one's mind	

Ken couldn't <u>decide</u> if he wanted an apple or an orange for lunch.

foolish (fü l´ish) without sense; not wise; like a fool

It was <u>foolish</u> for Brad to try and fight with someone who was so much bigger than himself.

goodness (gu̇d´nis) kindness

Abe Lincoln believed in the <u>goodness</u> of all men.

harm (härm) hurt

Rodney didn't want to <u>harm</u> the small puppy by moving him too much.

mistake (mis tāk´) error

The <u>mistake</u> cost Benny an "A" on his math test.

warn (wôrn) give notice to

Mrs. Brown wanted to <u>warn</u> the children about cheating on the test.

CTR C-37

FRIEND OR ENEMY?

Necessary Words

People

Mr. Griffin   is the invisible man's real name.

CTR C-37

FRIEND OR ENEMY?

It was very strange to see the food float in the air. It would disappear as Griffin ate it.

> ***Preview:***   1. Read the name of the story.
>   2. Look at the picture.
>   3. Read the sentences under the picture.
>   4. Read the first four paragraphs of the story.
>   5. Then answer the following question.
>
> You learned from your preview that the invisible man was
> ___ a. playing a trick on Dr. Kemp.
> ___ b. very strong.
> ___ c. hungry and thirsty.
> ___ d. being foolish.
>
>   *Turn to the Comprehension Check on page 46 for the right answer.*

Now read the story.

Read to find out what Dr. Kemp decides to do.

FRIEND OR ENEMY?

"I don't believe this," Kemp said. "Is this some kind of joke? How is this trick being done?"

"Don't be foolish, Kemp," the voice said. "It's no trick. I'm really invisible. I'll touch you."

Dr. Kemp felt fingers touch his nose and his mouth. Then, he felt strong hands grab his arms. The invisible man was hurting him.

"See, Kemp," the voice said. "I am invisible. I've put on your housecoat because I'm cold. And I've been shot. You must give me food and water. Then I can rest. Please, Kemp! I'm an old friend."

"A friend?" Dr. Kemp said. "I can *see* all *my* friends!"

"Don't you remember?" the voice said. "You and I went to school together. We were going to learn how to be doctors. You sat next to me in class. My name is Griffin."

"Griffin!" Dr. Kemp did remember a boy named Griffin. He remembered that Griffin had been a strange boy and that they had not been close friends.

"I remember you now," Dr. Kemp said. "Why are you invisible? How did you become invisible? And why did someone shoot you?"

"It's a long story, Kemp," the voice said. "I'm too tired to tell it now. Give me some food and water and let me sleep, and I'll tell you about it tomorrow."

Dr. Kemp thought this over. He didn't like the idea of Griffin staying in his house. He would never know what Griffin was doing. But this way, Dr. Kemp could keep an eye on him. He was sure that Griffin had done something wrong.

"Please, Kemp," the invisible man said. "You must help me."

"Okay," Dr. Kemp said. "I'll help you. But you must tell me what this is all about, first thing in the morning."

Dr. Kemp gave the invisible man food and water. It was very strange to see the food float in the air. It would disappear as Griffin ate it. If he hadn't seen it with his own eyes, Dr. Kemp wouldn't have believed it.

After dinner was over, Dr. Kemp took the invisible man upstairs and put him to bed.

"Thanks, Kemp," the invisible man said. "You're the only one who has been nice to me. It seems that there's no more goodness left in the world. But those who have hurt me will be very, very sorry."

"What does that mean?" Dr. Kemp asked him.

"Never mind," the invisible man said. "Let me warn you, Kemp. Don't try to call the police. It would be a mistake."

"I gave my word," Dr. Kemp said. "Good night."

Dr. Kemp went down the stairs to bed. But no matter how hard he tried, he couldn't fall asleep. There was a lot he had to think about, and he couldn't decide what to do.

The Griffin he had met in school was not the same person. He had changed. Now that he was invisible, any goodness he had before, had disappeared with his body. Dr. Kemp had a feeling that Griffin would do harm to people. He thought that maybe he had harmed someone this afternoon, and that's why he had been shot.

Dr. Kemp decided it would be a foolish mistake not to tell someone about the invisible man. He had to warn the police. He would need their help.

So before he went to bed, Dr. Kemp wrote a note. He had told the invisible man he would not tell the police tonight. But tomorrow, the police must know where the invisible man was staying.

Dr. Kemp put the note in his mailbox and turned out the light.

CTR C-37

FRIEND OR ENEMY?

COMPREHENSION CHECK

Choose the best answer.

> **Preview Answer:**
> c. hungry and thirsty.

1. Why do you think Griffin went to Kemp's house for help?
   ___a. He lived nearby.
   ___b. Kemp was not only a doctor, but an old friend, too.
   ___c. He liked the kinds of food the doctor cooked.
   ___d. He had a doctor's appointment.

2. Dr. Kemp and Griffin went to school together. They
   ___a. were very close friends.
   ___b. were very strange friends.
   ___c. didn't remember each other.
   ___d. were both going to be doctors.

3. Why didn't Dr. Kemp like the idea of Griffin staying at his house?
   ___a. He didn't have room in his house for another guest.
   ___b. He didn't like Griffin wearing his housecoat.
   ___c. He would never know where he was or what he was up to.
   ___d. He was eating up all the food in his house.

4. What gave Dr. Kemp the idea that Griffin had done something wrong?
   ___a. Griffin was invisible.
   ___b. Griffin had been shot.
   ___c. Griffin wouldn't answer his questions.
   ___d. Griffin kept asking for help.

5. First, Griffin and the doctor had a talk. Then, Dr. Kemp gave him some food and drink. Then,
   ___a. Dr. Kemp put Griffin to bed.
   ___b. Griffin went out for a walk.
   ___c. Dr. Kemp went out for a walk.
   ___d. Dr. Kemp went to bed.

6. What did Griffin mean when he told the doctor that it would be a "mistake" to call the police?
   ___a. It was late at night, and all the policemen would be sleeping.
   ___b. It would do no good, because no one would believe the doctor's story.
   ___c. He was warning him that there would be trouble if he did so.
   ___d. He was telling him that he wouldn't be his friend anymore.

7. Dr. Kemp decided that he had to warn
   ___a. the people in the town.
   ___b. the police, because he would need their help.
   ___c. all the other doctors in town.
   ___d. the mailman.

8. How did Dr. Kemp warn the police?
   ___a. He walked to the police station.
   ___b. He called them on the phone.
   ___c. He sent them a note.
   ___d. He had a friend bring a note to the police.

9. Another name for this story could be
   ___a. "Close Friends."
   ___b. "Kemp Remembers Griffin."
   ___c. "No Trust in an Old Classmate."
   ___d. "Friends Always."

10. This story is mainly about
    ___a. Griffin visiting an old schoolmate.
    ___b. a kind doctor who does not trust an old schoolmate.
    ___c. Griffin and an old friend remembering their school days.
    ___d. a kind doctor who makes a new friend.

Check your answers with the key on page 67.

This page may be reproduced for classroom use.

CTR C-37

FRIEND OR ENEMY?

VOCABULARY CHECK

| decide | foolish | goodness | harm | mistake | warn |

I. Sentences to Finish

Fill in the blank in each sentence with the correct key word from the box above.

1. I couldn't _____ which shirt to buy, so I bought a sweater instead.

2. It was _____ of me to think that I could get away with a lie.

3. A smoke alarm will _____ a family that a fire has begun.

4. Rabbits can cause _____ to the vegetables in your garden.

5. If it wasn't for the _____ of our kind neighbor, we might never have found our dog.

6. The teacher checked my spelling test and found that I had made only one _____ .

II. Crossword Puzzle

Use the key words from the box above to fill in the blanks in the puzzle.

Across

3. hurt
4. kindness
5. give notice to
6. make up one's mind

Down

1. without sense; not wise
2. error

Check your answers with the key on page 71.

This page may be reproduced for classroom use.

47

CTR C-38

THE INVISIBLE MAN'S STORY

PREPARATION

Key Words

hate	(hāt)	dislike very much 　　*Wendy knew it wasn't nice to <u>hate</u> anyone.*
master	(mas´ tər)	person who rules or commands people 　　*When Bob gave me his dog, I became its <u>master</u>.* become skillful at something 　　*Though the French language is hard to learn, I will <u>master</u> it.*
mirror	(mir´ ər)	a glass in which you can see yourself 　　*Kelly looked into the <u>mirror</u> to make sure that her hair looked good.*
nobody	(nō´ bod ē)	no one; no person 　　*Kim was so good, she knew that <u>nobody</u> could beat her at the game.*
spread	(spred)	scattered; distributed; sent further out 　　*Walter <u>spread</u> his good cheer every place he went.* 　　*Lucy <u>spread</u> her jelly on the bread.*
understand	(un´ dər stand´)	get the meaning of 　　*The problem was too hard for Pete to <u>understand</u>.*

THE INVISIBLE MAN'S STORY

Necessary Words

magician (mə jish´ ən)   person who uses magic
The magician waved his wand, and the dog disappeared.

visible (viz´ ə bl)   seen with the eyes
As the airplane climbed higher and higher, the town became less visible to the passengers.

First, the magician made the cat disappear. Then, he waved his wand and the cat became visible again.

CTR C-38

THE INVISIBLE MAN'S STORY

The invisible man began to laugh. Dr. Kemp knew he had done the right thing by writing the note. But would the police get here in time?

Preview:	1. Read the name of the story.
	2. Look at the picture.
	3. Read the sentences under the picture.
	4. Read the first four paragraphs of the story.
	5. Then answer the following question.

You learned from your preview that Griffin
___ a. wanted Dr. Kemp as his new helper.
___ b. was not feeling well.
___ c. did not want to tell Dr. Kemp his story.
___ d. was tired of wearing the doctor's housecoat.

Turn to the Comprehension Check on page 52 for the right answer.

Now read the story.

Read to find out how Griffin became invisible.

THE INVISIBLE MAN'S STORY

The next morning, Kemp woke up early and went downstairs. The invisible man was up. He had put on Kemp's housecoat again.

"I'm feeling good this morning, Kemp," the invisible man said. "Much better. And I've been thinking. You would make a good helper."

"Helper?" Dr. Kemp asked. "What do you mean?"

"I'm going to tell you the story of how I became invisible," said the invisible man. "Then I'll tell you how you are going to help me.

"It started when we were in school. I never wanted to be a doctor like you did. I wanted to be better. I wanted to do something no one else had done before. I wanted to be invisible.

"I read every book on how it might be done, and I spent all the money I had on the things I would need for my experiments. When I was very close to learning what I needed to know, I ran out of money. This made me very angry. So, I took money from my father."

"I can't believe it!" Dr. Kemp said. "Your own father?"

"Yes," answered the invisible man. "I needed the money and I didn't care where I got it. After more hard work, I thought I found the drink for becoming invisible. I gave the drink to a cat to see if it would work. The cat disappeared; except for his eyes. They wouldn't go away! The cat made so much noise, that I had to let him go. Just think, Kemp, out there is just a pair of eyes walking around."

The invisible man laughed. Dr. Kemp did not.

"Next, I took the drink myself," the invisible man told Dr. Kemp. "I gave myself more, so that my eyes would disappear, too. It was very painful, and I almost died. But when I looked in the mirror, I was gone. There was nobody there. Nobody! The mirror was empty. I had done it. I was invisible!

"But I soon found out that being invisible was not so good. I had to take off all my clothes, and when it was cold, I got sick a lot. It was hard to get food because people would always notice the food floating away, and they would scream.

"I got mad and robbed a magician. That's where I got my wig and toy nose. Then I covered my face with bandages. I also wore gloves, a hat, and dark glasses so that no one could tell that I was invisible. People thought that I had been in a fire. They were afraid of me. Nobody was nice to me. I began to hate being invisible, and I began to hate people.

"That's when I moved to Mrs. Hall's hotel. I wanted to see if I could learn how to become visible again. But everyone bothered me and wouldn't let me work. I robbed the church and made dumb Mr. Marvel help me. He ran away, and when I tried to get him, some man shot at me.

"They are all foolish, Kemp. They don't understand what I've done, but I will teach them. They will understand fear. I will become their master, and you're going to help me."

"I will not," Dr. Kemp said. "You are not well, Griffin. You need help."

"Yes, that's right. I need *your* help, Kemp. You will do what I say, for I am your new master. From now on, the invisible man will spread fear in every town. He will be everyone's master. I hate them all, Kemp. I will hurt anyone who tries to stop me."

The invisible man began to laugh. Dr. Kemp knew he had done the right thing by writing the note. But would the police get here in time?

"You will help me, Kemp, or I'll hurt you. No one can stop me!" shouted the invisible man. "The time to spread fear has begun!"

CTR C-38

THE INVISIBLE MAN'S STORY

COMPREHENSION CHECK

Choose the best answer.

Preview Answer:
a. wanted Dr. Kemp as his new helper.

1. Griffin told Dr. Kemp that his troubles began
   ___a. when he was a young boy.
   ___b. when he was in school.
   ___c. after his first experiments.
   ___d. after he ran out of money.

2. Griffin never wanted to be a doctor. He wanted
   ___a. to be better than a doctor.
   ___b. to be a scientist.
   ___c. to be visible.
   ___d. to be like his father.

3. Griffin wanted to be invisible because
   ___a. it would be so easy to get rich.
   ___b. he wanted to get his father angry.
   ___c. he could do his experiments in secret.
   ___d. he wanted to do something that no one had ever done before.

4. Griffin gave the 'drink' to his cat first, because
   ___a. the cat was thirsty.
   ___b. there wasn't enough 'drink' for the both of them.
   ___c. he wanted to see if the cat liked it.
   ___d. he wanted to see what the 'drink' would do before he drank it himself.

5. First, the cat was given the 'drink.' Then, Griffin took some. Next, Griffin
   ___a. looked in the mirror - and it was empty.
   ___b. looked in the mirror - and saw only his eyes.
   ___c. took off all of his clothes.
   ___d. got sick.

6. Griffin was soon to find out that being invisible
   ___a. was a lot of fun.
   ___b. was not so good.
   ___c. made him very happy.
   ___d. made everyone else happy.

7. People were afraid of Griffin because
   ___a. he looked and acted very strange.
   ___b. he wore dark glasses.
   ___c. he was always wearing gloves.
   ___d. he was foolish.

8. Because he felt that no one was nice to him, Griffin decided to
   ___a. become Dr. Kemp's master.
   ___b. run away.
   ___c. rob the churches in every town.
   ___d. become everyone's master.

9. Another name for this story could be
   ___a. "An Unhappy Man and the Life he has Chosen."
   ___b. "Griffin Tells his Life Story."
   ___c. "Griffin Rules the World."
   ___d. "Griffin's New Master."

10. This story is mainly about
    ___a. spreading fear in every town.
    ___b. how Griffin gets Dr. Kemp to be his helper.
    ___c. an evil man who is unhappy with himself, and who takes his anger out on everyone around him.
    ___d. how Griffin will discover the new 'drink' that will make him visible again.

Check your answers with the key on page 67.

This page may be reproduced for classroom use.

CTR C-38

THE INVISIBLE MAN'S STORY

VOCABULARY CHECK

| hate | master | mirror | nobody | spread | understand |

I. Sentences to Finish

Fill in the blank in each sentence with the correct key word from the box above.

1. Sometimes it is hard for me to _____ why my baby brother cries so much.

2. We _____ the good news that Mother was coming home from the hospital.

3. Math class is sometimes so hard, that I wonder if I will ever _____ it.

4. I sometimes feel that I could _____ my sister when she takes my things without asking.

5. When the teacher asked the class to be quiet, _____ said a word.

6. My friend and I made funny faces at each other in the _____ .

II. Using The Words

On the lines below, write six of your own sentences using the key words from the box above. Use each word once, drawing a line under the key word.

1. _____

2. _____

3. _____

4. _____

5. _____

6. _____

Check your answers with the key on page 71.

This page may be reproduced for classroom use.

CTR C-39

THE ESCAPE!

PREPARATION

Key Words

easily	(ēz´ l ē)	without trying hard 　　*The other team won the game <u>easily</u>.*
fool	(fül)	person without sense; person who acts unwisely 　　*Pat thought Nancy was a <u>fool</u> for not going out with Bob.*
intend	(in tend´)	mean to; plan 　　*Cindy didn't <u>intend</u> to make everyone sad.*
safety	(sāf´ tē)	being free from harm or danger 　　*Mr. Wilson made sure that everyone thought of <u>safety</u> while they were working.*
since	(sins)	because; from (a past time) till now 　　*There was no use fighting, <u>since</u> David was never wrong.* 　　*I haven't had a bubble bath <u>since</u> I was a little child.*
stupid	(stü´ pid)	not smart; dumb 　　*Pete was sure that Nick wasn't as <u>stupid</u> as everyone thought.*

CTR C-39

THE ESCAPE!

Necessary Words

downstairs   (doun´ stãrz´)   down the stairs
                                                    Bill slipped on a banana peel and fell <u>downstairs</u>.

CTR C-39

THE ESCAPE!

"Get him!" shouted Dr. Kemp. "Catch him before he escapes!"

Preview:	1. Read the name of the story.
	2. Look at the picture.
	3. Read the sentences under the picture.
	4. Read the first four paragraphs of the story.
	5. Then answer the following question.

You learned from your preview that Griffin
___ a. wanted to rule the world.
___ b. waited for the police to arrive.
___ c. told Dr. Kemp that he was a fool.
___ d. asked Dr. Kemp to call the police.

Turn to the Comprehension Check on page 58 for the right answer.

Now read the story.

Read to find out if the invisible man gets away.

THE ESCAPE!

Dr. Kemp now knew that Griffin was evil. The invisible man was going to spread fear in every town, and people would be hurt. Since he was invisible, no one could find him or stop him.

Dr. Kemp decided that he must stop the invisible man. He hoped the police had received his note. He would try and keep the invisible man at his house so the police could get him. He hoped the police were on their way.

"What do you intend to do?" asked Dr. Kemp. He wanted to keep the invisible man talking.

"Don't be a fool, Kemp!" the invisible man said. "I intend to rule the world. No one can stop the invisible man. They would be stupid to try."

"Do you think you can really rule the world?" Dr. Kemp asked. "No one will help you." He looked out the window to see if the police were coming.

"I can easily rule the world!" said the invisible man. "Who can keep me from doing it? And you will help me, Kemp, or you will be sorry."

There was a loud knock on the door downstairs.

"Who is that?" asked the invisible man. "Who is knocking?"

Dr. Kemp knew it was the police. He pushed the invisible man out of the way, then he ran downstairs and opened the door.

"Hurry!" he said to the police. "The invisible man is upstairs! Catch him before he escapes!"

The police ran upstairs. They saw Dr. Kemp's housecoat moving down the hall.

"Get him!" shouted Dr. Kemp.

One of the policemen grabbed the housecoat. "I've got him," a policeman shouted.

The other policemen tried to help catch the invisible man. But Dr. Kemp's housecoat dropped on the floor, and the police could no longer see where he was. All the policemen fell down. The invisible man had pushed them.

Dr. Kemp heard the invisible man run down the stairs. He saw his front door open.

"You are a fool, Kemp!" the invisible man shouted. "It was a stupid mistake... and you'll pay for it."

Dr. Kemp saw the door shut. He knew it was too late. The invisible man had escaped.

"What should we do now?" asked one of the policemen.

"This is very bad," Dr. Kemp said. "We must tell every person in every town to keep their doors and windows locked. The invisible man intends to spread fear everywhere. The safety of the people is in our hands."

The police left Dr. Kemp's house and went to every town. They warned the people about the invisible man. The people were scared when they heard what the police had to say, and they locked their doors.

But the invisible man could not be stopped. He attacked a man that very afternoon, hurting the man very badly.

The police went back to Dr. Kemp's house. They told him about the man who had been hurt by Griffin.

Dr. Kemp was very sad. He knew that the evil happenings were only beginning.

"I have more bad news," he told the police. "I got a note in the mail today. It was from the invisible man. He said that since I tricked him, he's going to hurt me. He said there is nothing I can do; that he will get me today."

"Then your safety is in our hands," a policeman said. "We will stay here with you."

"That's no good," said Dr. Kemp. "We must make a trap for the invisible man. We must catch him before he hurts anyone else."

The policemen knew Dr. Kemp was right. Dr. Kemp told them his plan.

"When the invisible man comes, we will be ready," said Dr. Kemp. "The time has come to stop the invisible man."

CTR C-39

THE ESCAPE!

COMPREHENSION CHECK

Choose the best answer.

> **Preview Answer:**
> a. wanted to rule the world.

1. Dr. Kemp kept the invisible man talking because
   ___a. he wanted to hear the rest of Griffin's story.
   ___b. he liked talking with the invisible man.
   ___c. it was too early to go to bed.
   ___d. it would give the police a chance to arrive.

2. If Kemp didn't keep Griffin talking, where do you suppose Griffin might go?
   ___a. Upstairs, to bed
   ___b. To a tavern for a drink
   ___c. To the store to buy a new housecoat
   ___d. Into the town to spread fear

3. When the police first arrived, they saw Griffin upstairs in the hall. Then, what did Griffin do so that he could not be seen?
   ___a. He left through the front door.
   ___b. He climbed out a window.
   ___c. He took off Kemp's housecoat.
   ___d. He hid under his bed.

4. What did Griffin mean when he told Kemp that he would 'pay' for his mistake?
   ___a. That the mistake would cost Kemp a lot of money
   ___b. That he would come back and break all his windows
   ___c. That he would return and hurt the doctor
   ___d. That he would never speak to him again

5. When the police went into the town to warn everybody about the invisible man,
   ___a. the people locked their doors.
   ___b. no one would believe their story.
   ___c. everyone left town.
   ___d. everyone laughed at the police.

6. After his escape, what did the invisible man do that very afternoon?
   ___a. He robbed another church.
   ___b. He returned to Kemp's house to eat.
   ___c. He attacked a man and hurt him very badly.
   ___d. He attacked a policeman.

7. How did Kemp find out that the invisible man was coming back to get him?
   ___a. Griffin sent the doctor a note.
   ___b. A policeman told him.
   ___c. Mrs. Hall called the doctor and told him.
   ___d. Griffin called him on the telephone.

8. Kemp and the policemen were planning to catch the invisible man. How were they planning to do this?
   ___a. They would catch him with a big net.
   ___b. They would set a trap for him.
   ___c. They would get him with attack dogs.
   ___d. They would give him the 'drink' to make him visible.

9. Another name for this story could be
   ___a. "The Invisible Man Gets Even."
   ___b. "Ruler of the World."
   ___c. "The Invisible Man Escapes Again."
   ___d. "Foolish Dr. Kemp."

10. This story is mainly about
    ___a. policemen who can't seem to do their job.
    ___b. how a kind doctor tries, but fails, to stop an evil man.
    ___c. everyone in town locking their doors and windows.
    ___d. Dr. Kemp's plan to stop Griffin.

Check your answers with the key on page 67.

This page may be reproduced for classroom use.

THE ESCAPE!

VOCABULARY CHECK

| easily | fool | intend | safety | since | stupid |

I. Sentences to Finish

Fill in the blank in each sentence with the correct key word from the box above.

1. I haven't been to the circus _____ I was a little child.

2. Bill was a _____ to think I would lie for him.

3. Seatbelts should be worn for the _____ of all passengers.

4. I do not _____ to go to the dance on Saturday.

5. The team worked so hard, that the game was _____ won.

6. Bob played a _____ trick on me, so I got him back.

II. Read each sentence. Then find which key word beneath it could be used instead of the underlined word or words. Circle the letter in front of the correct key word.

1. I didn't <u>plan</u> to forget your birthday.
   a. fool b. intend c. since d. easily

2. Mary passed her spelling test <u>without trying hard.</u>
   a. since b. stupid c. easily d. fool

3. Pete did something that was <u>not smart,</u> and everyone laughed.
   a. stupid b. easily c. safety d. since

4. <u>Because</u> I was late, I had to stay after school.
   a. Easily b. Since c. Intend d. Fool

5. We do not run in the halls for our own <u>freedom from harm or danger.</u>
   a. since b. fool c. safety d. easily

6. Because she acts like a <u>person without sense</u>, she hasn't many friends.
   a. stupid b. since c. safety d. fool

Check your answers with the key on page 71.

This page may be reproduced for classroom use.

CTR C-40

VISIBLE AT LAST

PREPARATION

Key Words

somehow	(sum´hou)	in a way not known; in one way or another Dick knew that, <u>somehow</u>, he would prove his point.
struggle	(strug´l)	great effort; hard work It was a <u>struggle</u> to get through the tough homework we had today.
through	(thrü)	from end to end; into and out of The little child ran <u>through</u> the house, screaming.

trouble	(trub´l)	disturb; a problem; worry
		    Mike didn't want to <u>trouble</u> his mother, so he made his own lunch.
		
		    Tom didn't want to cause <u>trouble</u> for his brother by telling a lie.
		
		    I didn't want to <u>trouble</u> Mother, so I came home on time.

unless	(un les´)	except that There was no way they could get to the dance <u>unless</u> someone drove them.
yet	(yet)	up to now Kathy knew that the party hadn't started <u>yet</u>, so she took her time getting ready.

CTR C-40

VISIBLE AT LAST

Necessary Words

choke (chōk) stop the breath of an animal or person by squeezing the throat
The robber began to choke the man when he wouldn't hand over his money.

CTR C-40

VISIBLE AT LAST

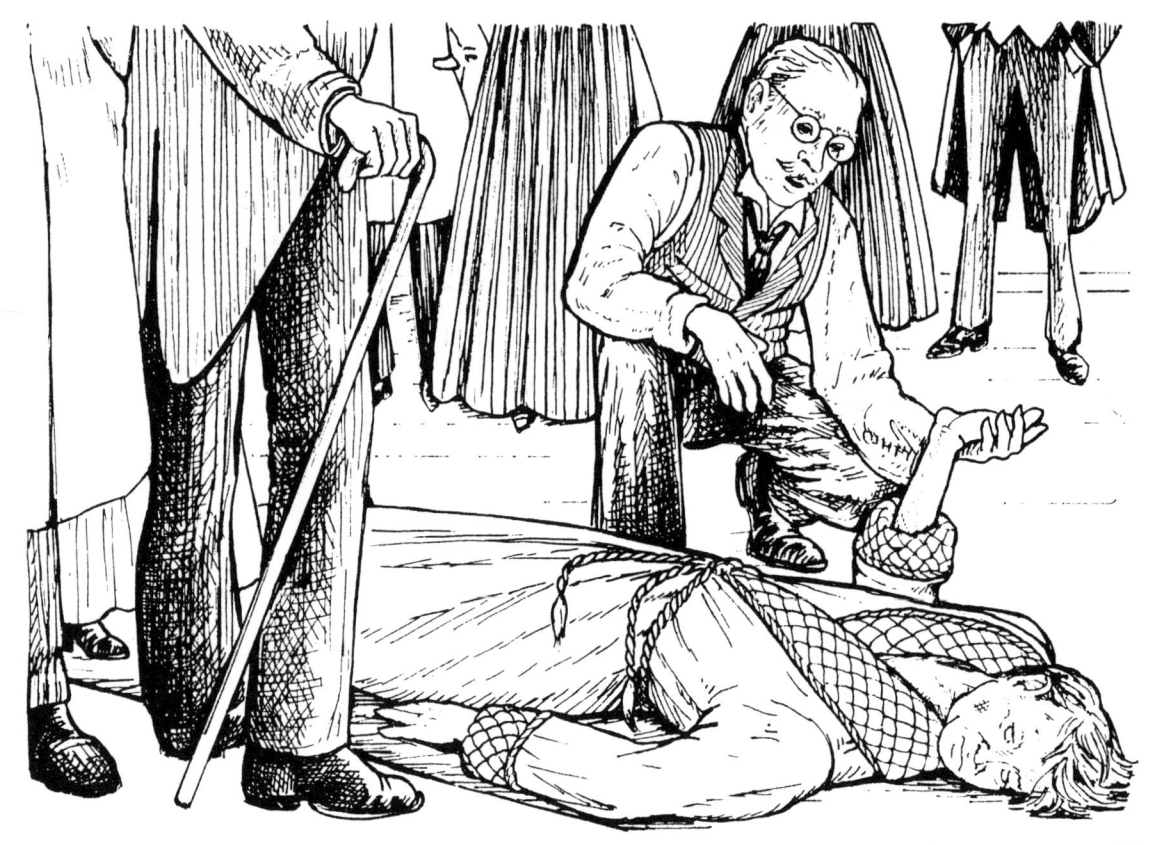

Dr. Kemp was sorry that they didn't catch him alive, but there had been no other way to stop him.

Preview:	1. Read the name of the story.
	2. Look at the picture.
	3. Read the sentence under the picture.
	4. Read the first paragraph of the story.
	5. Then answer the following question.

You learned from your preview that
___ a. Griffin struggled for his life.
___ b. Griffin had to be caught, or Kemp would die.
___ c. Dr. Kemp was going to beat up Griffin.
___ d. Dr. Kemp struggled with Griffin.

Turn to the Comprehension Check on page 64 for the right answer.

Now read the story.

Read to find out how the invisible man is caught.

VISIBLE AT LAST

Dr. Kemp sat in his house waiting for the invisible man. He knew that if he did not stop the invisible man, he would be hurt, and a lot of other people would be hurt, too. Dr. Kemp knew that his struggle with Griffin was a struggle for life or death. Somehow, he must beat the invisible man.

The police were outside hiding. When the invisible man got there, they would come out and catch him. Everyone was very scared. Unless they caught the invisible man, he would cause trouble everywhere.

They heard a window break. The invisible man was there, yet they couldn't see him. He had thrown a rock at the window.

Dr. Kemp heard the window break, too. He ran into the room and saw a rock that had come through the window. He knew the invisible man was there.

One of the policemen went to Dr. Kemp's door. "You've got trouble, doctor," the policeman said. "The invisible man is here."

Then the policeman fell back. It looked like he was fighting with the air, but he was really fighting with the invisible man.

As they struggled, somehow, the invisible man got the policeman's gun. Dr. Kemp watched the fight from his window. He saw the gun float up in the air. The policeman stopped fighting. There was no way to stop the invisible man if he had a gun.

Dr. Kemp grabbed a bat and ran downstairs. He heard the invisible man break another window.

The other policemen came running into Dr. Kemp's house. There was a big fight that went through the whole house. Dr. Kemp saw the gun floating through the air. He knew it was the invisible man. He hit the gun with the bat and knocked it out of the invisible man's hand.

"I will get you yet, Kemp!" the invisible man screamed.

The trouble was that no one could see the invisible man. Then a chair went flying in the air, almost hitting Dr. Kemp. Kemp knew that this was not the way to get the invisible man. He would have to make the invisible man leave the house.

"You'll never catch me, Griffin," Dr. Kemp said. "Your days of fear are almost over."

Then Dr. Kemp ran out of the house. He ran to the town as fast as he could. It wasn't long before he heard the invisible man running behind him.

They ran a long time. Dr. Kemp was getting very tired. Unless he made it to the town and got help, the invisible man would win.

Dr. Kemp finally made it to the town. But he didn't stop running. "Help me," he shouted. "Help me catch the invisible man!"

The people of the town ran out of their houses. They formed a long line at the end of the street. When Dr. Kemp made it to the line, the people went all around him. Dr. Kemp and the invisible man were now in the circle. Kemp knew that the invisible man could not get away.

Dr. Kemp felt hands around his neck. The invisible man was trying to choke him. Dr. Kemp fought with the invisible man.

The people watching the struggle rushed in to help Kemp. Soon, many were holding on to the invisible man. They began to hit him with all their might. They were angry for all the trouble he had caused.

Soon, Dr. Kemp shouted, "Stop! He is no longer fighting."

The crowd moved away, and right before their eyes, the invisible man became visible! At last, they could see him.

Dr. Kemp could see that Griffin had been beaten up very badly. He grabbed Griffin's hand, knowing that he was dead.

Dr. Kemp was sorry that they didn't catch Griffin alive, but there had been no other way to stop him. Griffin could have been a great doctor, but he decided to harm people; not help them. And now, it was all over.

"It's done," Dr. Kemp said to the crowd. "There is no need to fear him anymore. The invisible man is no more."

CTR C-40

VISIBLE AT LAST

COMPREHENSION CHECK

Choose the best answer.

Preview Answer:
b. Griffin had to be caught, or Kemp would die.

1. Dr. Kemp sat in his house, waiting for the invisible man. The police
   ___a. waited outside.
   ___b. loaded their guns.
   ___c. broke a window.
   ___d. hid in the bushes.

2. When Dr. Kemp heard the window break, he knew that
   ___a. the kids from down the street had broken it.
   ___b. the invisible man had returned to get him.
   ___c. the police were warning Kemp that Griffin was there.
   ___d. trouble was everywhere.

3. First, the invisible man got the policeman's gun. Then, Kemp grabbed a bat. Next,
   ___a. Kemp hit Griffin with the bat.
   ___b. Kemp struggled with a policeman.
   ___c. Griffin grabbed the bat and hit Dr. Kemp.
   ___d. Kemp knocked the gun out of Griffin's hand.

4. Kemp knew that the only way to get Griffin was to
   ___a. make him leave the house.
   ___b. make him something to eat.
   ___c. keep on fighting until Griffin gave up.
   ___d. kill him with his bat.

5. As fast as he could, Kemp ran out of the house to the nearest town. Why?
   ___a. Griffin was chasing him with the gun.
   ___b. Griffin was chasing him with the bat.
   ___c. He wanted to see how fast Griffin could run.
   ___d. He wanted Griffin to follow him out of the house.

6. When Kemp made it to town, why did the people form a circle around him?
   ___a. They hoped to trap Griffin in the circle.
   ___b. They wanted Dr. Kemp to stop running.
   ___c. They wanted to protect Dr. Kemp.
   ___d. They wanted to play a game.

7. The invisible man tried to kill the doctor by
   ___a. choking him with the bat.
   ___b. choking him with a rope.
   ___c. putting his hands around Kemp's neck.
   ___d. firing the gun.

8. After the fight, the crowd watched the invisible man
   ___a. cry.
   ___b. disappear.
   ___c. become visible.
   ___d. bleed to death.

9. Another name for this story could be
   ___a. "The Big Fight."
   ___b. "The Invisible Man Returns."
   ___c. "A Happy Town."
   ___d. "Free at Last."

10. This story is mainly about
    ___a. an evil man who brings harm to everyone and, finally, to himself.
    ___b. an evil man who gets even with a friendly doctor.
    ___c. Dr. Kemp's struggle with life and death.
    ___d. how a crowd beat a man to death.

Check your answers with the key on page 67.

This page may be reproduced for classroom use.

CTR C-40

VISIBLE AT LAST

VOCABULARY CHECK

| somehow | struggle | through | trouble | unless | yet |

I. Sentences to Finish

Fill in the blank in each sentence with the correct key word from the box above.

1. I wasn't sure how I would finish all my work, but, _____ , I would manage.

2. I wouldn't dive in the pool _____ Jim dived in first.

3. Because I caused some _____ in school, Mother wouldn't let me out to play.

4. A bird flew _____ my bedroom window.

5. It was not a _____ to eat all the cookies.

6. Dinner wasn't ready _____ , so I didn't have to go inside.

II. True or False?

Put an X next to TRUE if the sentence makes sense. Put an X next to FALSE if the sentence does not make sense.

1. When you struggle for an answer to a question, you are sure you know the answer. ___ True ___ False

2. When you go through a door, you are entering or leaving a place. ___ True ___ False

3. If your car gives you trouble, it means your car runs well. ___ True ___ False

4. If your friends won't do something unless you do, it means they want you to do something also. ___ True ___ False

5. If you haven't done your homework yet, it means it hasn't been done up to now. ___ True ___ False

6. If you look for an answer somehow, it means you will look for the answer in one way or another. ___ True ___ False

Check your answers with the key on page 72.

This page may be reproduced for classroom use.

NOTES

COMPREHENSION CHECK ANSWER KEY
Lessons CTR 304-31 to CTR 304-40

LESSON NUMBER	1	2	3	4	5	6	7	8	9	10	PAGE NUMBER
CTR C-31	d	c	a	◇b	b	○d	a	○d	△a	□a	10
CTR C-32	c	○b	◇d	c	b	○d	◇a	d	△c	□d	16
CTR C-33	◇c	a	b	d	d	○a	c	○b	△a	□b	22
CTR C-34	b	b	d	◇a	○b	○d	○a	c	△c	□d	28
CTR C-35	○b	○d	a	◇a	c	○c	a	a	△b	□d	34
CTR C-36	b	d	a	○b	◇b	a	d	b	△c	□d	40
CTR C-37	○b	d	○c	b	◇a	○c	b	c	△c	□b	46
CTR C-38	b	a	d	○d	◇a	b	○a	d	△a	□c	52
CTR C-39	d	○d	c	○c	a	c	a	b	△c	□b	58
CTR C-40	a	○b	◇d	a	○d	○a	c	c	△d	□a	64

◇ = Sequence (recalling order of events in the story)

○ = Inference (not said straight out, but you know from what is said)

△ = Another name for the story

□ = Main idea of the story

67

NOTES

VOCABULARY CHECK ANSWER KEY

Lessons CTR C-31 to CTR C-40

LESSON NUMBER		PAGE NUMBER
31	THE STRANGE MAN	11

I.
1. fierce
2. blind
3. bother
4. scared
5. everybody
6. skin

II. Crossword:
- 1 Across: scared
- 2 Down: everybody
- 3 Across: blind
- 3 Down: bother / Down from 1: skin
- 4 Across: fierce

32 FLYING FURNITURE! 17

I.
1. robber
2. church
3. puzzle
4. scream
5. pretend
6. peek

II.
1. scream, e
2. robber, d
3. pretend, f
4. peek, b
5. church, a
6. puzzle, c

33 INVISIBLE! 23

I.
1. loose
2. escape
3. crowd
4. disappear
5. stare
6. touch

II.
1. YES
2. NO
3. NO
4. YES
5. NO
6. NO

VOCABULARY CHECK ANSWER KEY

Lessons CTR C-31 to CTR C-40

LESSON NUMBER		PAGE NUMBER

34 THE UNHAPPY HELPER   29

I. 1. mad
    2. notice
    3. slap
    4. fear
    5. attack
    6. helper

II.
```
Z  U  H  M  A  D  V  R  S
O  T  E  W  N  S  P  Q  L
Q  B  L  E  D  B  Z  X  A
G  H  P  F  O  X  F  T  P
A  F  E  N  O  T  I  C  E
V  E  R  X  N  Z  A  V  X
L  A  T  T  A  C  K  L  T
S  R  P  W  X  Y  A  N  Y
```
(MAD, SLAP, NOTICE, ATTACK, FEAR, HELPER circled)

35 MORE FEAR IN A NEW TOWN   35

I. 1. poke
    2. cheek
    3. finger
    4. polite
    5. teeth
    6. speed

II. 1. b
    2. b
    3. a
    4. b
    5. a
    6. b

36 DR. KEMP'S VISITOR   41

I. 1. forward, darkness
    2. shoot, seize
    3. upstairs, shake
    4. upstairs, darkness
    5. forward, seize
    6. shake, shoot

II. 1. shake, c
    2. forward, f
    3. upstairs, d
    4. darkness, a
    5. shoot, b
    6. seize, e

VOCABULARY CHECK ANSWER KEY

Lessons CTR C-31 to CTR C-40

LESSON NUMBER		PAGE NUMBER

37 FRIEND OR ENEMY? 47

I.
1. decide
2. foolish
3. warn
4. harm
5. goodness
6. mistake

II.

```
        ¹f
         o
         o
         l
         i
         s
        ³h a r ²m
               i
      ⁴g o o d n e s s
               t
              ⁵w a r n
               k
            ⁶d e c i d e
```

38 THE INVISIBLE MAN'S STORY 53

I.
1. understand
2. spread
3. master
4. hate
5. nobody
6. mirror

39 THE ESCAPE! 59

I.
1. since
2. fool
3. safety
4. intend
5. easily
6. stupid

II.
1. b
2. c
3. a
4. b
5. c
6. d

71

VOCABULARY CHECK ANSWER KEY

Lessons CTR C-31 to CTR C-40

LESSON NUMBER   PAGE NUMBER

40   VISIBLE AT LAST   65

I.
1. somehow
2. unless
3. trouble
4. through
5. struggle
6. yet

II.
1. FALSE
2. TRUE
3. FALSE
4. TRUE
5. TRUE
6. TRUE